LIFEHACKS
FOR KIDS

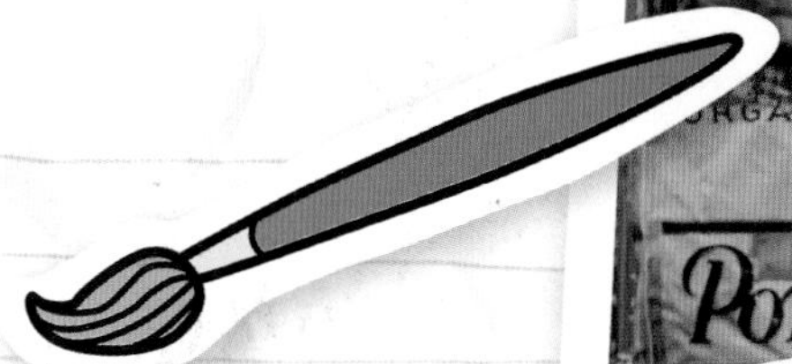

Created by Jeannie Roshar and Gary Anthony Williams

www.hmhco.com

Illustrations by Artful Doodlers, LTD.

ISBN 978-1-328-74213-1

Manufactured in China

SCP 10 9 8 7 6 5 4 3 2 1

4500661967

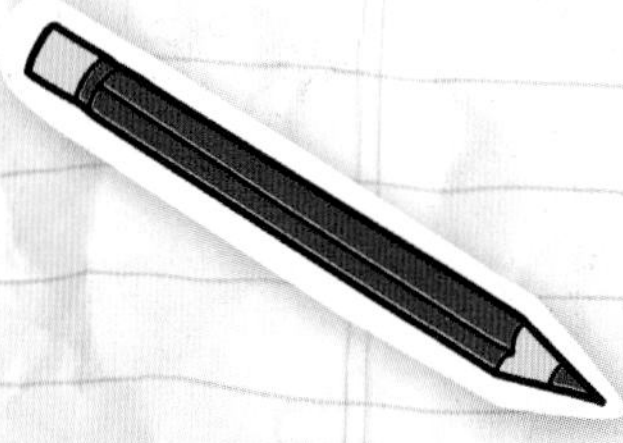

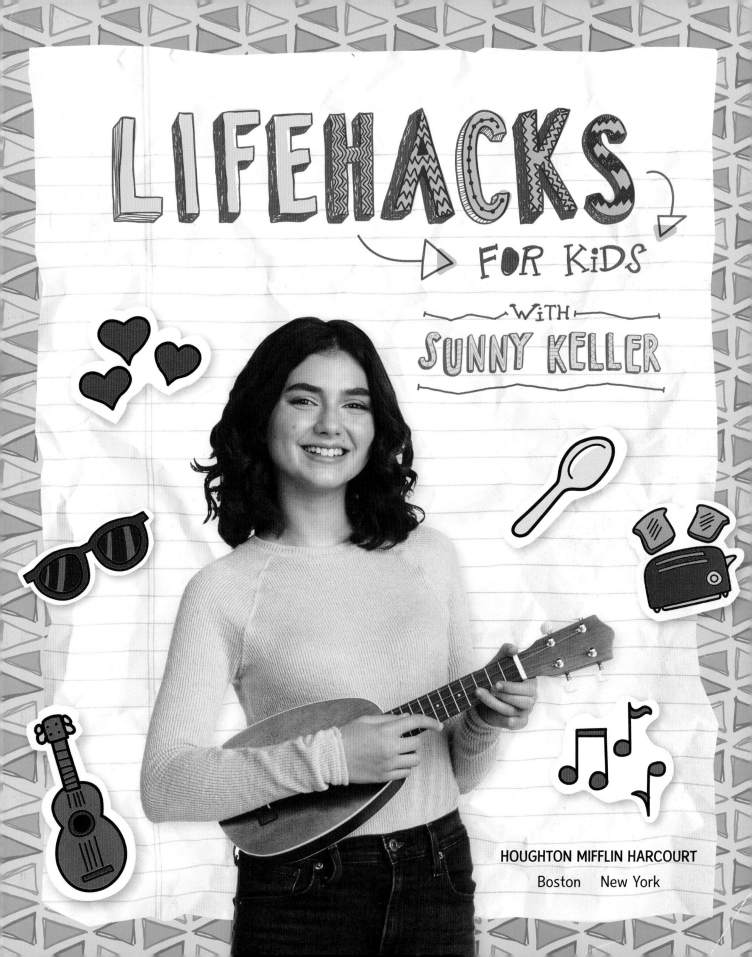

LIFEHACKS

FOR KIDS

WITH

SUNNY KELLER

HOUGHTON MIFFLIN HARCOURT

Boston   New York

CONTENTS

ABOUT THIS BOOK

Hi!! I'm Sunny Rae Keller, the host of the DreamWorksTV show *Life Hacks for Kids* on YouTube. You may already know my show, but once you read this book, I hope you'll be hooked . . . and hacking away very shortly.

To make it easy for you, I've divided the book into different sections with easy-to-follow hacks from the show in each one. The hacks are written like recipes in a cookbook. First I'll tell you what you need to round up and have on hand, and then I'll give you step-by-step directions with photos so you can easily follow along. Want to know the best part? You can do these hacks in any order you'd like! Try them whenever the mood hits you—for holidays, for gift giving, if you're having a snack attack, if you want to decorate your room, if you want to make something special for yourself, or for no reason at all except to have fun!

At the end of each section, I answer some questions so you can learn more about me, my family, my life at school, what my favorite things are, and stuff like that.

How *Life Hacks for Kids* Got Started

I come from a pretty crafty family. My mom is an artist, and my dad is a musician and writer. I've always loved to make crafts with my mom. A few years ago, I started a business called All Dolled Up. I fixed my friends' dolls and made clothes for them. I guess you could say that was my first real experience as a professional crafter.

I also loved making hair bows out of old napkins. One day, I decided to post a video of myself creating these hair bows on my YouTube channel. At that time, I didn't have any followers. A friend of my family's saw the video and showed it to some people at DreamWorksTV. They liked it and ordered a couple of episodes, and my show took off from there! I was eleven when *Life Hacks for Kids* started, and that was three years ago.

Filming Each Episode of the Show

I get a lot of help putting the show together. I work with a really great film crew. Each episode of *Life Hacks for Kids* is three to four minutes long. We film four episodes in one day. It takes two or three hours to film each episode. So to shoot four of them, it takes all day! We do this once a month on a Sunday, so I don't miss any school. A new episode of the show airs once a week.

So what goes into the making of an episode? I work with two directors, Jeannie Roshar and Gary Anthony Williams, and we brainstorm together on the hacks.

I practice making the hacks a few days before the show so I can get them right during filming. Two cameras are used during filming—Camera A and Camera B. One is used to shoot the wide shots, and the other camera is always focused on my hands. There's also a boom pole and a monitor. The room is pretty small, but we make it work.

Once the show is shot, Dustin Hahn, the film editor, edits the episode. My mom is my PA (production assistant) on the show. She basically just acts like my mom. Hosting *Life Hacks for Kids* is a lot of work, but I love the crew and I love shooting the show.

So now please enter my world—welcome to *Life Hacks for Kids*!

— SUNNY KELLER

HACKTIVITIES

IF YOU'VE GOT NOTHING TO DO, WELL, I'VE GOT A COUPLE OF TRICKS FOR YOU. SO TAKE A LOOK AT THESE VIDS, 'CAUSE IT'S *LIFE HACKS FOR KIDS.*
—SUNNY

You know those kinds of days—you're bored, it might be raining outside, you don't have anything to do, you may be home with a friend or your sister or brother, but you're tired of playing the same old games—well, cheer up! Here are some hacktivities for you to try.

In this chapter, you will find:

* ⁂ **BOTTLE BOWL-A-RAMA**

* ⁂ **INDOOR SOCCER GAME**

* ⁂ **PING-PONG PAN**

* ⁂ **MEGA BOSS EMOJI TOSS**

PLAY ALONE OR WITH YOUR FRIENDS OR FAMILY, AND CHASE THOSE BOREDOM BLUES AWAY!

BOTTLE BOWL-A-RAMA

Want to go bowling? You can make your own indoor bowling alley with my Bottle Bowl-a-Rama.

YOU'LL NEED:

- different-colored acrylic paints (I used 3 colors)
- 6 plastic water bottles
- 1 ball
- water (optional)

1. Squirt a small amount of paint inside each bottle.

TIP: If your paint is really thick, you can add about 1 teaspoon of water as well.

2. Put the cap back on the bottle and shake it until the paint coats the inside. Do this with all of your bottles.

3. Take the caps off and let
the bottles dry overnight.

4. The next morning, put the caps
back on, and you're ready to roll!

5. I'm about to bowl a strike!
Better use a bigger ball.

THE CROWD GOES WILD!

WOO-HOO!

HOPE YOU ENJOY YOUR
BOTTLE BOWL-A-RAMA.

19

INDOOR SOCCER GAME

You love to play soccer, but you know you can't play in your house, right? Well, now you can. Here's my cool Indoor Soccer Game.

YOU'LL NEED:

- 1 pizza box
- 1 pair of scissors
- green construction paper
- tape
- 6 bendy straws
- white marker
- 1 cotton ball or Ping-Pong ball

1. On opposite sides of your pizza box bottom, cut slits and bend down flaps. These will be your goals. Make sure they're big enough for the ball to fit through—about 6 inches across.

2. Now put down the green construction paper for the grass.

TIP: If your construction paper isn't wide enough to line the entire pizza box, overlap one sheet of paper onto another and use tape to hold them together.

3. Next, flatten and fold the long end of a bendy straw. This part can be tricky, so just stay with it!

21

4. Insert the folded end into the long end of another straw.

5. Bend the tiny ends to form goalposts.

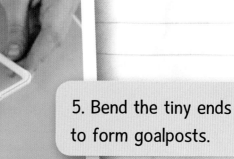

6. Tape the straw goalposts in front of one of the goals you just cut out. Repeat steps 4 through 6 for the goal at the opposite side of the box.

7. Finally, draw markings in white to make your field look official.

8. To play, blow the ball back and forth with straws. And remember, it's a lot more fun when you play with a friend.

9. Before you know it, you'll be a pro like me!

PING-PONG PAN

Let's play Ping-Pong with my Ping-Pong Pan!

YOU'LL NEED:

- 12 plastic cups
- 1 muffin tin
- 1 pair of scissors
- sticky notes
- marker
- 1 Ping-Pong ball

1. Place the plastic cups into the muffin tin.

2. Next, cut out squares from the sticky notes. Make sure the glue stripe is at the top of each square.

25

3. Write numbers on the notes and stick them to your cups. NOTE: The numbers will be your point values.

4. Finally, grab a Ping-Pong ball and get bouncing!

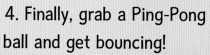

THREE POINTS!

I'M A NATURAL AT THIS STUFF!

HOPE YOU ARE TOO!

MEGA BOSS EMOJI TOSS

Using my EMOJInation, I came up with this game. It's my Megaboss Emoji Toss. Hope your "heart eyes" like it.

YOU'LL NEED:

- 1 black marker
- 1 pair of scissors
- yellow, black, and red felt
- 1 hot glue gun
- beans or any other type of filling
- cardboard box
- knife
- spray paint (optional)

1. To make a beanbag, draw and cut out two circles about 6 inches in diameter from the yellow felt.

2. Hot-glue them together around the edges, leaving an opening about 3 inches long. (You'll use this to fill the bag with beans.)

TIP: Be careful. The glue gun is hot!

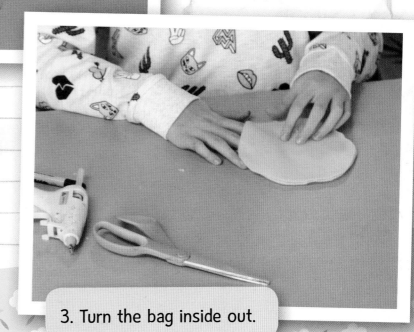

3. Turn the bag inside out.

4. Cut the features to make an emoji face from the other colors of felt.

5. Hot-glue the pieces onto the beanbag.

6. Now fill the bag with beans and glue it closed.

7. Repeat steps 1 through 6 to make a few more emoji bags.

8. Next, take the cardboard box and, using the knife, cut it at an angle to make the sloping target.

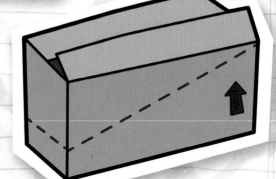

TIP: You may want to get an adult's help with this.

9. Turn the box upside down and cut three target holes about 10 inches across in the cardboard.

10. Decorate the box with spray paint if you want.

11. Add a number to each target hole for scoring. Play with a friend or two.

THESE HACKS MAKE ME FEEL LIKE AN EMOJI-GENIUS!

AN EMOJINIUS! I JUST INVENTED A WORD!

I AM A GENIUS! AND SO ARE YOU!

WE INTERRUPT THIS BOOK FOR A WORD WITH SUNNY

Q: What is your favorite activity?

A: I love playing the ukulele. I do that in my spare time.
I also love going to coffee shops and writing.
I live next door to my favorite coffee shop, so I'll go there to write or to do my homework.

Q: Which do you prefer—indoor or outdoor activities?

A: I think that really depends. I live in Southern California, where it's constantly hot. It doesn't get below seventy degrees here. I like indoor activities, as I said, going to coffee shops or just hanging out. I do love being outside, though—at the beach or walking around.

Q: What do you like to write?

A: I like writing poetry. I'm trying to write my own songs. It's hard, but I'm trying. I like writing stories and screenplays, and I also like turning my screenplays into short movies.

Q: Who do you like to be with the most—one friend or a group of friends?

A: I have a group of five friends at school. I have other friends, but this is my main group of friends. They're in my classes. It is also fun being one-on-one with a friend. But I like being in a group better.

Q: What's your favorite activity to do with your friends?

A: Making films! I use my friends as actors. They help me on the set, and I help them with their movies. It's a big collaboration. I just love making films. It's my favorite thing to do, and it's really fun!

HACK THAT SNACK ATTACK

It's that time of the day. You're hungry! You need a snack. What's in the house? What will satisfy those hunger pangs?

In this chapter, you will find some of my favorite recipe hacks. They're easy, and they're yummy!

✷ **INSIDE-OUT INDOOR S'MORES**

✷ **SAUSAGE-A-GHETTI**

✷ **ONE-HAND PANCAKES**

✷ **FIVE-MINUTE FREEZY CREAM**

✷ **TWO INGREDIENTS SWEET BREAD**

MAKE THESE FOR YOURSELF, YOUR FAMILY, OR YOUR FRIENDS. HAPPY SNACKING!

INSIDE-OUT INDOOR S'MORES

Love s'mores? Now you can have them whenever you want them. Here's my recipe for Inside-Out Indoor S'mores.

YOU'LL NEED:

- marshmallows
- graham crackers
- mini chocolate chips

HERE'S WHAT TO DO:

1. Make a small hole in the center of a marshmallow.

2. Now break a graham cracker into small pieces.

3. Push a few of the pieces into the hole.

4. Then fill up the rest of the hole with mini chocolate chips.

CHOC CHIPS

5. Make several of these.

INSIDE-OUT INDOOR S'MORES.

CHOCOLATY CRACKERS ON THE INSIDE,

MARSHMALLOW ON THE OUTSIDE,

DELICIOUSNESS
ALL AROUND.

SAUSAGE-A-GHETTI

Uh-oh! Tummy's growling. That can mean only one thing. It's time for a special treat—my Sausage-a-Ghetti.

YOU'LL NEED:

- 1 knife
- sausage or hot dogs (I use veggie dogs)
- uncooked spaghetti
- pot of boiling water
- salt

SEA SALT

SPAGHETTI

SAFETY SUNNY HERE. Since we're using a stove and a knife, you might want to get an adult's help with this hack.

HERE'S WHAT TO DO:

1. Using the knife, slice the sausage or hot dog into little disks.

2. Next, poke a piece of uncooked spaghetti through one of the sausage disks.

3. You can thread more than one piece of spaghetti into each sausage disk.

PING!

4. Have an adult cook your mealtime masterpiece in boiling salted water for about 10 minutes, then drain it.

DELICIOUS!

ONE-HAND PANCAKES

The days of eating breakfast with two hands are over, thanks to this new invention, the stick! Prepare to be amazed by my One-Hand Pancakes.

YOU'LL NEED:

- pancake batter
- 1 empty squeeze bottle (optional—see Tip)
- 1 skillet
- Popsicle sticks
- 1 spatula

TIP: I hacked my batter by putting it in a squeeze bottle.

HERE'S WHAT TO DO:

1. We're using a stove, so you might want to get an adult's help. Pour (or squeeze) a small amount of pancake batter into the skillet.

2. Place a Popsicle stick onto the batter.

3. Add a little more batter on top of the stick.

4. Then cook like normal: let the pancake cook until bubbles form on the surface.

5. Using the spatula, carefully flip the pancake.

6. My one-hand pancakes. And with my free hand, I'll conduct a symphony. Soothing and delicious.

FIVE-MINUTE FREEZY CREAM

This wonder of nature will cool you down lickety-split! It's my Five-Minute Freezy Cream.

YOU'LL NEED:

- ½ cup milk or cream

- 2 sandwich-size resealable plastic bags

- 1 tablespoon sugar

- ¼ teaspoon vanilla extract

- 6 tablespoons sea salt

- 1 gallon-size resealable plastic bag

- ice

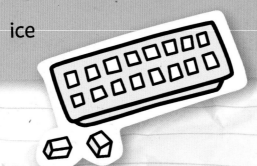

1. Pour the milk or cream into a sandwich-size resealable plastic bag.

2. Add the sugar.

3. Add the vanilla extract.

4. Then double bag it in the other sandwich-size resealable bag to be extra safe.

5. Put the salt into the gallon-size resealable bag.

6. Fill it halfway with ice cubes.

SCIENCE TIME! Salt lowers the freezing point of water, which will help turn this cream into ice cream in record time!

7. Put the bag of cream inside the bag of ice and close it up.

8. Shake, shake, shake your way to deliciousness!

9. In about five minutes, you'll be ready to chill out. You worked hard. You deserve some ice cream!

TWO INGREDIENTS SWEET BREAD

Here's a tasty after-party treat! It's my Two Ingredients Sweet Bread.

YOU'LL NEED:

- 2 cups melted ice cream (I'm using Chocolate Chip!)
- 1 mixing bowl
- 1½ cups self-rising flour
- 1 wooden mixing spoon
- 1 bread pan
- cooking spray

1. Make sure the ice cream is soft. Pour it into the mixing bowl.

2. Add the flour and mix it together with the spoon.

55

3. Spray the bread pan with the cooking spray, so your sweet bread won't stick, then pour your batter into the pan.

4. Have an adult bake it at 350°F for about 40 minutes.

PING!

PASSES THE SMELL TEST.

AND IT DEFINITELY PASSES THE TASTE TEST!

STAY TUNED: SUNNY ANSWERS MORE QUESTIONS

Q: Wonderful hacks, Sunny! Your readers would love to know—what is your favorite snack?

A: I love avocados so much! My favorite snack is avocado toast. I can eat it anytime of day.

Q: Mmmm, sounds delish! What's the recipe?

A: It's simple. I make toast, mush avocado onto it, add olive oil, salt, and a spice called zatar. Delicious!

Q: Are your parents good cooks?

A: My mom is a great baker, and my dad is a terrific cook. My sister is good at both.

Q: What is your favorite thing to bake?

A: I like baking cookies with my sister. Gidget is four years younger than me, but she knows what she's doing—she's in control. I just follow what she does.

Q: Do you have any other siblings?

A: No, Gidget is my only sibling.

Q: You used veggie dogs in your Sausage-a-Ghetti hack. Are you a vegetarian?

A: Yes, I've been a vegetarian for five years, and I turned the rest of my family vegetarian too.

HACKCYCLE

I always try to keep the three Rs in mind when I create my hacks—reduce, reuse, and recycle. Here are some hacks that will make you feel good about reusing and recycling old things to create new things. Some will look great in your room, and some will be fun for play.

In this chapter, you can make:

* **A GROOVY LAVA LAMP**

* **BEANBAGS FOR THE FUNTASTIC PIZZA BOX BEANBAG TOSS (OR FOR JUGGLING OR PLAYING OTHER GAMES)**

* **A FUNTASTIC PIZZA BOX BEANBAG TOSS**

* **A SPOONTASTIC PLASTIC MIRROR**

ENJOY!

GROOVY LAVA LAMP

H₂O my goodness! What am I going to do with this empty water bottle? Why recycle when you can *hack*cycle? Here's my Groovy Lava Lamp.

YOU'LL NEED:

- 1 empty water bottle

- vegetable oil

- water

- food coloring

- 1 antacid tablet (like Alka-Seltzer)

HERE'S WHAT TO DO:

1. Fill the bottle about three-quarters full with vegetable oil.

2. Fill the rest of the bottle almost to the top with water.

3. Next, add 5 to 10 drops of food coloring.

TIP:
Try all kinds
of colors!

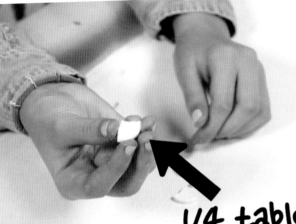

1/4 tablet

4. Break the antacid
tablet into quarters.

5. Drop one piece of the
tablet into the water.

Watch science do its work!

GROOVY, MAN.
TOTALLY GROOVY.

WHO KNEW YOU COULD DO SO
MUCH WITH A WATER BOTTLE?

BEANBAGS FOR THE FUNTASTIC PIZZA BOX BEANBAG TOSS

Here's how to make beanbags for the Funtastic Pizza Box Beanbag Toss.

YOU'LL NEED:

- 9 balloons
- 1 funnel
- about 1½ cups dry rice and beans
- 1 pair of scissors

1. Blow up one of the balloons to stretch it. Then let the air out.

2. Place the balloon over the small end of the funnel.

3. Using your funnel, fill the balloon up with beans and rice until it's about the size of a tennis ball.

4. Cut a little piece off the top of the balloon.

5. Fold the top over so the beans don't come out. Blow up another balloon to stretch it and let the air out again.

6. Then cut off the tip.

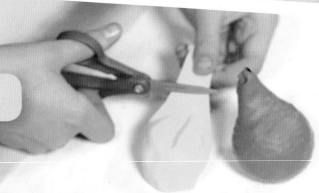

7. Next, slip that balloon over the beanbag. Finally, blow up a third balloon, let the air out, cut off the tip, and slip it over the beanbag.

8. Make two more beanbags the same way.

YOU CAN JUGGLE WITH THESE BEANBAGS, TOO.

FUNTASTIC PIZZA BOX BEANBAG TOSS

Here's a game that's loads of fun. It's my Funtastic Pizza Box Beanbag Toss.

YOU'LL NEED:

- 1 pen or pencil
- 1 cup
- 1 pizza box
- 1 knife
- duct tape
- 3 beanbags (see page 68)

1. Trace the cup twice onto the bottom of a pizza box.

2. Use the knife to cut out the holes.

TIP: Be careful with that knife! Get a parent to help out.

3. Cut off the lid of the pizza box, leaving about a 5-inch flap.

4. Turn the box over and use the flap to prop it up.

5. Tape the flap in place.

6. Grab your beanbags, and you're ready to play.

BEANBAG TOSS CHAMPION

YES! I'M A BEANBAG TOSS CHAMPION!

75

SPOONTASTIC PLASTIC MIRROR

Here's a hack that's fantastic and made out of plastic. I call it my Spoontastic Plastic Mirror.

YOU'LL NEED:

- 1 plastic lid about 8 inches in diameter (or you can use a paper plate)
- 1 pen or pencil
- 1 piece of cardboard
- 1 pair of scissors
- 1 small round mirror
- bunch of plastic spoons (the cheaper ones are the easiest to cut)
- 1 hot glue gun
- spray paint in your choice of background color
- paint in another color of your choice
- 1 paintbrush

HERE'S WHAT TO DO:

1. Use the lid to trace a circle on the cardboard.

2. Cut it out.

3. At the center of the circle, trace around your mirror to draw another circle.

4. Cut it out.

77

5. Now cut the handles off the spoons.

6. Starting on the outside, hot-glue a ring of spoons around the rim of the cardboard.

TIP: Be careful. The glue gun is HOT.

7. Keep gluing rings of spoons as you move to the center.

8. Once you're done, spray-paint the spoons and let them dry.

9. Then paint a design using the second color. Let it dry.

10. Finally, hot-glue the mirror in place.

THESE SPOONS SURE LOOK GOOD AND CAN MAKE YOU LOOK GOOD, TOO!

BREAKING NEWS: MORE WORDS WITH SUNNY

Q: It's great that you reuse and recycle old items into new ones on your show. How do you come up with your hacks?

A: Right, reusing and recycling is so important! Sometimes, I come up with the hacks, and sometimes my directors do. Other times, we'll find inspiration online and put our own twist to it. We're always sharing our ideas with each other.

I made this purse out of an old Skittles wrapper!

Q: Do you have a locker at school? Have you hacked your locker?

A: Yes, I actually do. Lockers are fun. I love decorating mine. This is my last year at middle school, and I've decorated it every year. I take wrapping paper with cute designs on it, then cut it to the size of the locker and use it as locker wallpaper. I keep the paper up with magnets or tape so it's easy to take down at the end of the year. I hang photos on the wallpaper with more magnets, and I add sticky notes too.

Q: Do you have a favorite recycling or reusing hack?

A: Let's see. There are so many hacks. But I definitely love this one. We did an episode of candy wrapper hacks. I made a purse out of a candy wrapper. It even has a zipper. It came out so cute. I use it every day. It looks really good. You wouldn't know it was made from a candy wrapper.

Q: Where do you go to school, and what subjects do you take?

A: I go to a Cinematic Arts School in Los Angeles. I take regular classes—math, science, history, and English. But since it's a performing arts school, I take a dance class for physical education.

I also study filmmaking. Filmmaking is my favorite class.

Q: What hack do you think everyone should know?

A: I don't think I have a specific one. But if there's something you're hesitant about throwing away, you can always make it into something new. Recycle your things. Don't just throw them out. You can always make them into another new, exciting, and creative item.

NIFTY THRIFTY GIFT HACKS

> I have learned that people (and pets) appreciate homemade gifts, so I usually try to make my own presents for special occasions.

In this chapter, there are instructions for making gifts for Dad, Mom, siblings, friends, dogs, and cats. You will find the following hacks:

* **MAKE-A-MUG**

* **DELIGHTFUL DUCT TAPE EARRINGS**

* **MELT-YOUR-HEART MELTED HEART ART**

* **ROLY-POLY TREAT BALL**

* **PERFECT PULL TOY**

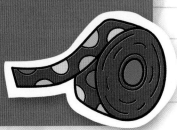

EVERYONE WILL BE IMPRESSED BY YOUR THOUGHTFUL GIFTS!

MAKE-A-MUG

My Make-a-Mug hack is a gift for Dad that he's sure to love.

YOU'LL NEED:

- different color bottles of nail polish
- 1 big plastic container full of water
- 1 toothpick
- 1 plain mug
- permanent markers

1. Pour some nail polish into the water.

TIP: Mix all kinds of colors.

2. Swirl the polish with the toothpick to create a marble effect.

3. Dunk the bottom half of the mug into the nail polish and water. The marbled pattern will stick.

4. Let the mug dry upside down.

5. Once it dries, write a colorful message with your permanent markers. Make it personal so your dad knows it's just for him.

THE MAKE-A-MUG—WITH A PERSONAL TOUCH THAT DAD'S GOING TO LOVE.

DELIGHTFUL DUCT TAPE EARRINGS

Whether it's for a birthday or a holiday, gifts can get pretty expensive. But nothing says love like a great hacked present! Here's something for Mom, your sisters, or other girls in your life— my Delightful Duct Tape Earrings.

YOU'LL NEED:

- colorful duct tape
- 1 pair of scissors
- 1 thumbtack
- ear wires from an old pair of earrings

1. Fold a piece of duct tape in half.

2. Cut the tape into a feather shape.

3. Cut slits to make your design even more feather-like.

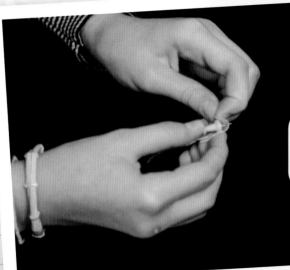

4. Poke a hole at the top of the feather with the thumbtack.

5. Hook the ear wire through the hole.

6. Repeat the process to make your second earring.

DEEEEEE-LIGHTFUL!

MELT-YOUR-HEART MELTED HEART ART

Here's a hack that will melt your heart. In fact, it's called Melt-Your-Heart Melted Heart Art!

- 1 pencil
- 1 sheet of paper
- 1 pair of scissors
- 1 canvas
- crayons
- 1 hot glue gun
- drop cloth or newspapers
- 1 hairdryer

94

HERE'S WHAT TO DO:

1. Draw a heart on your sheet of paper.

TIP: To make your heart symmetrical, fold the paper in half and draw one side of the heart with the fold at the middle!

2. Cut out the heart.

3. This will be your stencil.

4. Place the stencil in the center of the canvas.

5. Now lay your crayons around the stencil with the sharpened ends pointing out. I'm making a rainbow pattern.

6. Hot-glue the crayons to your canvas. Make sure you don't glue the stencil.

TIP: Be careful! The glue gun is hot.

7. Once the crayons are dry, put down a drop cloth (or newspapers) to protect your work area.

8. Remove the stencil from the center.

9. Turn your hairdryer on at full power.

TIP: You might want an adult to help you with this part.

10. Use the hairdryer to melt the crayons. Hold the canvas up and point the dryer downward, so the wax spatters away from the heart shape at the center.

11. Rotate your canvas as you melt each crayon.

A MELTY MASTERPIECE! C'EST BON——MELTIFIQUE!

ROLY-POLY TREAT BALL

I love cats, but I don't have one. So my dog Ginger will play the role of GiGi, the cat. Here's how you can make a Roly-Poly Treat Ball for your cat.

GINGER!

YOU'LL NEED:

- 1 pair of scissors
- 1 empty toilet paper roll
- cat treats

HERE'S WHAT TO DO:

1. Cut the toilet paper roll into five skinny strips.

2. Pick the best four.

3. Insert one strip into another so that it crosses like this.

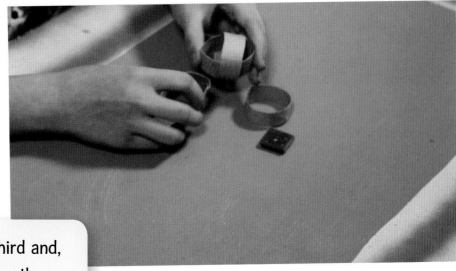

4. Add the third and, finally, the fourth.

Cat Treat

5. There, you have your ball.

6. Add in a few of your cat's favorite treats.

YOUR CAT WILL LOVE BATTING THIS AROUND TO GET THE TREAT OUT.

RIGHT, GIGI? YOU'RE WELCOME!

PERFECT PULL TOY

Ginger is a playful dog. But dog toys can be really expensive unless you know this simple hack for the Perfect Pull Toy!

YOU'LL NEED:

- 1 pair of scissors
- 3 old T-shirts
- duct tape (optional—see Tip)

1. Cut three strips off the bottom of each T-shirt. I used three different-colored shirts, but you can use whatever you like.

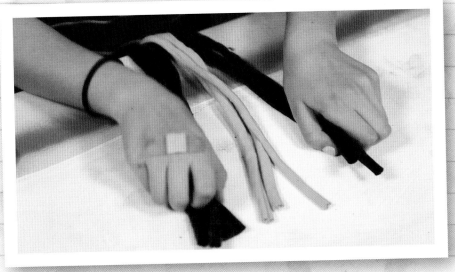

2. Separate the nine strips into groups of three.

3. Place the strips together and tie them in a big knot near one end.

4. Braid them.

TIP: Tape the knot to the end of the table to make braiding easier.

5. When you're done, tie another knot at the end of your braided rope.

NOW YOUR PERFECT PULL TOY IS READY FOR ACTION! HERE, GINGER!

Q: What is one gift you've given that your receiver has loved?

A: I gave my mom a pair of earrings that I hacked out of a plastic bottle. She wears them every day. She loves them. They go great with her outfits. They look really good on her.

Q: What's one of your favorite gift hack ideas?

A: Sometimes it's really special to make your own packaging for a gift. I like to make a gift box out of paper. It's similar to an origami box, but then I decorate it and make it my own. You can put any gift you make (or buy) into it and give it as part of the gift.

Q: How many pets do you have?

A: I have four dogs.

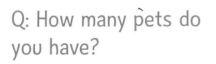

Q: Wow, four dogs! What are their names?

A: Max, Ginger, Millie, and Biscuit. They're all rescue dogs. Max is a corgi. He's the only boy, and he's our oldest. Ginger is a Chihuahua. Millie is a terrier. And Biscuit—we have no idea what kind of dog she is.

Q: Your dog Ginger plays the role of GiGi the cat in your Roly-Poly Treat Ball hack. Do you have a cat?

A: No, my entire family is allergic to cats.

HACK YOUR ROOM

Whether you share a bedroom or have your own, it's great to surround yourself with things that you love and to put a lot of your personality into your space.

In this chapter, you will find instructions to make:

* ⁕ **HANGING BASKETS O' BEAUTY**

* ⁕ **YES, I CAN-CAN PLANTER**

* ⁕ **TERRIFIC TERRARIUM**

* ⁕ **HACKED HEADBAND HOLDER**

AHHH! TO LIVE CLUTTER-FREE, TO BE ORGANIZED, AND TO BE SURROUNDED BY BEAUTIFUL PLANTS! WHO COULD ASK FOR MORE?

HANGING BASKETS O' BEAUTY

Gotta lotta stuff and no dresser top or countertop space? Not a problem when you make my Hanging Baskets o' Beauty!

YOU'LL NEED:

- 1 pair of scissors
- some cord
- 3 small decorative buckets

1. Cut two pieces of cord about five times the width of a bucket.

2. Double one of the strings by folding it in half.

3. Feed it through the handle of a bucket and pull the loose ends through the loop to secure it.

4. Now tie the loose ends to the right and left sides of another bucket at the handles.

5. You've connected two buckets.

6. Now use another string to connect these two buckets to the third bucket.

7. You've made a chain of buckets.

LOTIONS, NAIL STUFF, AND HAIR STUFF . . . ALL ORGANIZED AND HANGING ON A WALL.

YES, I CAN-CAN PLANTER

Let's get growing with my Yes, I Can-Can Planter!

YOU'LL NEED:

- 1 old, clean can
- sticker paper
- 1 pair of scissors
- stickers
- potting soil
- 1 plant

1. Remove the old label from the can.

Use can to make a line in the sticker paper for easy cutting.

TIP

2. Cut the sticker paper to fit around the outside of the can.

3. Stick it to the can.

TIP

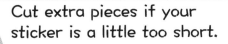

Cut extra pieces if your sticker is a little too short.

4. Decorate with stickers.

5. Place some soil and the plant inside the can. Make another planter, if you like.

THE PERFECT PLANTERS FOR THE PERFECT PLANET!

TERRIFIC TERRARIUM

Let's hack a Terrific Terrarium out of a CD case.

YOU'LL NEED:

- 1 empty plastic cup
- a handful of potting soil
- water
- 1 plastic spoon
- 1 CD case
- grass seeds
- clear tape

HERE'S WHAT TO DO:

1. In a cup, mix the potting soil and water with the spoon until it's nice and wet.

2. Open the CD case and take out the plastic piece that holds the CD.

3. Fill the CD case about a third of the way with the soil and water mixture.

121

4. Next, near the top of the soil, sprinkle some grass seeds, or any other seeds you'd like to see grow.

5. Now close the case.

6. Seal the bottom and sides with tape. Finally, put it in a sunny window, and watch Mother Nature do her work.

7. In two to three days, the seeds will start to look fuzzy, and in ten days, they'll look like this:

TERRARIUMIFFIC!

Terrariumiffic!

HACKED HEADBAND HOLDER

Oh, no! Too many headbands, and not enough holding space. What's a poor hacker to do? Hacking Powers, hacktivate! Time for my Hacked Headband Holder!

YOU'LL NEED:

- 2 rolls of paper towels
- several yards of fabric
- 1 hot glue gun
- 1 pair of scissors
- 2–3 feet of ribbon
- 4 flower decorations large enough to cover the end of a paper towel roll

HERE'S WHAT TO DO:

1. Lay a roll of paper towel on the fabric.

2. Hot-glue one side of the fabric to the roll.

3. Cover the entire roll of paper towel with the fabric.

TIP: Be careful! The glue gun is hot!

4. Cut off the extra fabric.

5. Hot-glue the loose end of the fabric.

6. Glue the fabric inside the tube at one end of the roll.

7. Repeat on the other side.

TIP: Glue in both sides.

8. Make a second fabric-covered roll.

9. Cut a piece of ribbon about 8 inches long, add glue to each end, and use it to attach the two rolls together on one side.

10. Do the same on the other side of the two rolls.

11. Now cut another piece of ribbon about 18 inches long and glue each end to one side of the top roll so you can hang your holder.

12. Finally, glue one flower decoration to each end of the paper towel rolls to cover the holes.

ALL DONE! BAND-TASTIC!

LET'S TAKE A COMMERCIAL BREAK AND SPEAK WITH SUNNY

Q: Do you have your own bedroom, or do you share one with your sister?

A: We recently moved into a new house. Before that, I shared a room with my sister. But now we have our own separate rooms.

Q: What does your room look like?

A: My room still needs a few more decorations. I think we're going to paint it soon.

I don't have a bed frame yet. I have a mattress that's very low to the ground. The dogs love it because they can easily get up on it.

There are lots of windows. I have a desk and a walk-in closet. My room isn't huge, but it isn't tiny either. I really love it. It has string lights, which give it a very homey feel.

Q: When you do paint it, what color do you think you will choose?

A: I'm not sure yet. Maybe pastel colors. I like coral colors and blues as well. My favorite colors are navy and green, but I think I'd go with a lighter color for my room.

Q: Do you decorate your room with any of the hacks that you make on the show?

A: I have the rainbow fan that I made on one of my shows, and I keep that in my room. When it spins, you see a rainbow.

I also have some of the frames that I hacked on my show. I have a camera, and I love to take pictures. So I've put photos in the frames and placed them on the walls of my room.

Q: Do you wear clothes from your own closet for the videos?

A: Yes! I use my own wardrobe. I try to make sure that I don't wear the same thing too often!

THE ARTS HACKS

I love to sing, dance, play musical instruments, draw, write, and make films.

In this chapter, I've put together some of my favorite music, art, and dancing hacks. You will find:

* EASY AS 1-2-3-D ART HACK

* SCREEN PRINTING STAMP

* JAMAICAN STEEL DRUMS

* BEAUTIFUL BELLS BRACELET

* HACKITY TIPPETY TAPPITY

YOU SHOULD BE ABLE TO WHILE AWAY THE HOURS AND MAKE BEAUTIFUL MUSIC AND ART AND HAVE FUN DANCING!

EASY AS 1-2-3-D ART HACK

I just got a new pair of 3-D glasses. Hmm! Not exactly what I thought they'd be. Luckily, I know a 3-D marker hack that's so good, you won't even need glasses. I call it the Easy as 1-2-3-D Art Hack!

YOU'LL NEED:

- 1 pencil
- 1 sheet of paper
- your hand
- markers

1. Use your pencil to lightly trace your hand on the paper.

2. Now use a marker to draw a straight line from one side of the paper to the outline of your hand.

3. When you come to the outline, draw an arch over to the other side of your hand.

4. Then draw a straight line to the other side of the paper.

5. Continue this pattern. Use multiple colors to make your drawing even more eye-catching.

6. Arch the fingers and thumb as well.

7. This takes a while, but it's totally worth it! When you're done, it looks like your hand is coming right off the paper, and it's as easy as 1-2-3!

I THINK I'LL ENTER MY DRAWING INTO THE REMARKERABLE ART SHOW!

SCREEN PRINTING STAMP

Here's an easy way to make a Screen Printing Stamp.

- 1 pair of scissors

- 2 foam plates or containers

- 1 paintbrush or pencil

- paint

- 1 paint roller

- 1 sheet of paper

138

1. Cut a flat piece from a foam plate or container to whatever shape you want.

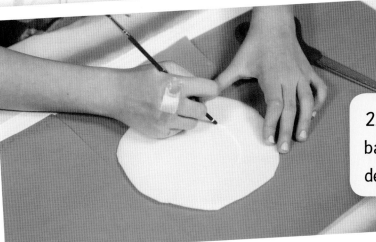

2. Next, using your pencil or the back of your paintbrush, draw a design on the piece of foam.

TIP: If your design includes words, be sure to write them backwards.

3. Press down hard enough to make deep grooves in the foam, but try not to press all the way through.

4. Now pour some paint into the second plate and put an even coat of paint on the paint roller.

5. Roll the paint onto your foam plate design.

6. Gently press a sheet of paper on top of the design.

AND THERE YOU HAVE IT! THE COOL PART IS, YOU
CAN USE THIS STAMP OVER AND OVER AGAIN.
YOU CAN EVEN PRINT IT ON T-SHIRTS. FANTASTICO!

JAMAICAN STEEL DRUMS

There's only one thing better than making music. That's making your own musical instruments. And even better than that, you can hack musical instruments from around the world. Today's hack: Jamaican Steel Drums!

YOU'LL NEED:

- different sizes of empty cans
- rubber bands
- 2 pencils for drumsticks

1. Arrange the cans upside down in a cluster, placing the larger ones in the center.

2. Place the smaller cans on the outside. The more sizes you have, the better!

3. Now tie rubber bands together.
You need a long string of them.

TIP

→

Make a long string of rubber bands!

It has to fit around all the cans.

4. Wrap the string of rubber bands around the cans.

5. Secure it with a double knot.

Double knot!

IT'S TIME TO BURN THE NOISE! YEAH, MON! THE SOUND OF THE ISLAND! BEAUTIFUL AND LOUD!

BEAUTIFUL BELLS BRACELET

Ahhh! I hear a bell ringing, and that bell rings a bell! Let's make my Beautiful Bells Bracelet.

YOU'LL NEED:

- thick elastic
- 1 pair of scissors
- assorted ribbons
- elastic string
- about 13 small bells

1. Measure the thick elastic to fit your wrist.

2. Now trim it.

3. Tie a knot and cut off the extra pieces of elastic.

4. Next, cut some ribbon pieces to the length you want them to hang. I made mine about 8 inches long.

5. Tie the ribbons onto the elastic band—keep adding ribbons until it's full.

6. Tie one end of the elastic string to the bracelet.

7. Thread the bells onto the elastic string. I used 13 bells.

8. Wrap the bell string all around the band, distributing the bells evenly.

9. When you get to the end, tie the bell string to itself. Cut off any extra elastic.

SOUNDS REAL SWEET. YOU CAN WEAR THEM ON YOUR WRISTS OR EVEN YOUR ANKLES.

HACKITY TIPPETY TAPPITY

I love to dance. But tap shoes can be expensive, unless you know this simple hack that I call Hackity Tippety Tappity.

YOU'LL NEED:

- a pair of old shoes
- about 18 pennies
- 1 hot glue gun

HERE'S WHAT TO DO:

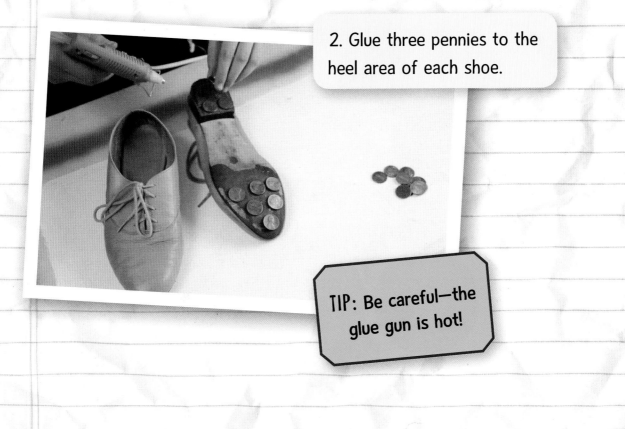

1. Hot-glue about six pennies to the toe area on the bottom of each shoe.

2. Glue three pennies to the heel area of each shoe.

TIP: Be careful—the glue gun is hot!

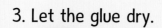
3. Let the glue dry.

YOU'LL BE DANCING UP A STORM IN NO TIME!

152

LET'S CUE SUNNY

Q: How many instruments do you play?

A: I play three—mainly, the ukulele. And I can play a little bit of guitar and violin.

Q: How long have you been playing these instruments?

A: I've been playing the ukulele since I was seven, and the other two instruments since I was ten.

Q: You said your mom is an artist and your dad is a musician and writer. Do they play musical instruments?

A: My dad plays the guitar, and he sings. He also writes songs. My mom mostly focuses on art.

Q: And Gidget, is she interested in the same things?

A: Gidget loves art. She's a great artist. She's also a great writer. She hasn't gotten into music yet, but she's a great cook.

Q: Did you take lessons, or are you self-taught?

A: I never took lessons to learn how to play any of these instruments. A friend of mine in school played the ukulele. I became friends with him, and his dad gave me a ukulele and taught me how to play a few things on it. Then I just went from there. The guitar is similar to the ukulele, so I picked it up, but I'm still learning.
I was also in the school orchestra in fifth grade.

Q: Do you have a favorite musician or a favorite type of music?

A: Yes, my favorite musician is Regina Spektor. I've always loved her. She's amazing! I just saw her in concert for the first time, and when I did, I cried because I was so happy!

I like alternative music—not exactly rock, not exactly pop. I don't really listen to the radio or to popular pop songs. I grew up listening to the Beatles, David Bowie, Queen—all these bands that my dad loves. Now I have a taste for that kind of music as well as alternative music.

Q: I know you've done some tap dancing on *Life Hacks for Kids*. What kind of dancing do you enjoy?

A: I love dancing, but it's not what I dedicate my life to. I used to do tap dancing—nothing advanced—and ballet too. Now I do hip-hop dancing. I take hip-hop lessons once a week—just for fun, to be with my friends, and for exercise.

Q: What are your favorite art projects?

A: I love doodling. I like watercolors. I love drawing and sketching.

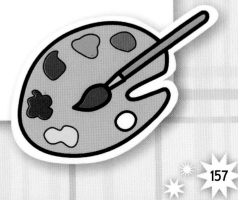

HACKS FOR ALL SEASONS

Ahhh! The four seasons! Each one brings something different. Do you have a favorite season?

In this chapter, you will find one hack for each season—summer, fall, winter, and spring!

* **NOODLE SPRINKLER**

* **NATURALLY NATURAL JEWELRY TREE**

* **HO HO SNOW**

* **COOL COLORFUL COTTON SWAB BOUQUET**

I HOPE YOU GET OUT THERE (OR STAY IN) AND ENJOY THE SEASONS!

NOODLE SPRINKLER

I'm using my noodle right now. Literally. Here's my hack for a Noodle Sprinkler!

YOU'LL NEED:

- 1 pool noodle
- 1 chopstick
- 1 plastic bottle cap
- duct tape
- 1 pair of scissors
- 1 garden hose

1. Poke lots of holes all around the pool noodle using the chopstick.

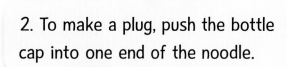

2. To make a plug, push the bottle cap into one end of the noodle.

3. Tape over the plug
end of your noodle.

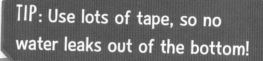
TIP: Use lots of tape, so no
water leaks out of the bottom!

4. Slide the end of the hose into
the open end of the noodle.

5. Push the hose in a few inches so it stays inside the noodle.

NOW TURN ON THE HOSE AND PREPARE
FOR MAXIMUM SUNNY DAY FUN!

NATURALLY NATURAL JEWELRY TREE

Need a really cheap and unique way of organizing your jewelry? Here's my Naturally Natural Jewelry Tree.

YOU'LL NEED:

- a few small tree branches

- 1 vase or bottle

- spray paint

1. Choose a few small branches with lots of places to hang your jewelry.

2. Break off smaller twigs at the bottom of each branch.

3. Decorate the branches
with any color of spray paint.

4. After they dry, place the
branches into the vase.

5. Then hang your necklaces, bracelets, and even your rings.

ISN'T NATURE BEAUTIFUL?

HO HO SNOW

Let's make snow with my Ho Ho Snow hack.

YOU'LL NEED:

- 1 box of baking soda
- 1 large bowl
- 1 can of shaving cream
- 1 large spoon

HERE'S WHAT TO DO:

1. Dump the entire box of baking soda into the bowl.

2. Now slowly add the shaving cream.

HO! HO! HO! I'M SUNNY CLAUS!

3. Mix the baking soda with the shaving cream using the spoon . . .

4. . . . until it starts looking and feeling like snow.

5. You can even use your hands, if you'd like.

SEE? IT LOOKS LIKE SNOW. IT EVEN FEELS COLD LIKE SNOW. AND THE BEST PART IS YOU CAN MAKE A SNOWBALL.

AND THAT'S HOW YOU MAKE HO HO SNOW. I EVEN MADE A LITTLE SNOWMAN, AND WE'LL BE BEST FRIENDS FOREVER.

COOL COLORFUL COTTON SWAB BOUQUET

My table is looking pretty plain lately. Time to pep it up with my Cool Colorful Cotton Swab Bouquet.

YOU'LL NEED:

- cotton swabs
- 1 pair of scissors
- foam balls
- food coloring
- water
- 1 bowl
- protective gloves
- stems from old plastic flowers (or some twigs)
- 1 vase

HERE'S WHAT TO DO:

1. Cut several cotton swabs in half.

2. Poke the cut ends into a foam ball.
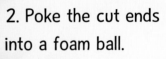

3. Cover the ball with as many cotton swabs as you'd like.

4. Now mix the food coloring and water in the bowl.

TIP: Try all kinds of colors!

5. Wearing the protective gloves, roll the ball in the bowl of food coloring and water. Let the cotton swabs soak up the color.

6. Remove the leaves and other pieces from the plastic flower stems (or twigs).

Strip everything off the plastic flower stems.

7. Poke a stem into the foam ball.

8. Make as many flowers as you'd like. Let them dry and put them in the vase.

YOU'RE ALL DONE!

Q: This may be a difficult question, because you live in California, but what is your favorite season?

A: I love fall. It's my favorite season. I wish that fall happened here, but it doesn't. I was born in Chicago, and I love being in New York City in the fall.

I love tea and sweaters and rain, which is ironic, because my name is Sunny.

Q: So you were born in Chicago. When did you move to California?

A: We moved to California when I was two, so I'm growing up here.

Q: It might be hard for you to say that you have a favorite winter activity or summer activity, but do you?

A: I love going to the beach in the summer, and I love ice skating in the winter when there's fake snow. In California, you need to skate on fake snow!

LET'S GET PRANKED HACKS

I love to laugh and giggle and smile! What better way to do this than to prank your family and friends . . . as long as it's all in good fun!

HA HA HA!

HA HA HA!

HA HA HA!

In this chapter, you will find:

✳ **THE OLD KETCHUP & MUSTARD ON YOUR SHIRT FAKE-OUT HACK**

✳ **MAGICAL MILK SPILL**

✳ **BIG OL' LUMP O' COAL**

✳ **INVISI-PAINT**

HOPE YOU HAVE LOTS OF FUN!

THE OLD KETCHUP & MUSTARD ON YOUR SHIRT FAKE-OUT HACK

Two of my favorite condiments. Perfect for making one of my favorite ha-ha hacks. I call this one the Old Ketchup & Mustard on Your Shirt Fake-Out.

YOU'LL NEED:

- 1 empty plastic ketchup bottle
- red nylon string
- 1 pair of scissors
- 1 empty plastic mustard bottle
- yellow nylon string

HERE'S WHAT TO DO:

1. Cut the red string so it's a few inches longer than the ketchup bottle and its top.

2. Tie a big knot to one end of the red string.

3. Feed the cut end through the top of the bottle, starting from the inside.

4. Tie a small knot to keep the string from falling back through the hole.

5. Pull the string so that almost all of it is in the bottle and screw on the lid. Repeat the process with the mustard bottle and yellow string.

NOW WHEN YOUR FRIEND ASKS YOU TO PASS THE KETCHUP AND THE MUSTARD BOTTLES, SQUEEZE THE BOTTLES AND LET 'EM HAVE IT!

FAKE OUT!

BULL'S-EYE!

MAGICAL MILK SPILL

This hack is deliciously funny. I call it my Magical Milk Spill. But you won't need any magic or milk for it.

YOU'LL NEED:

- white nail polish
- 1 small plastic bag
- 1 pair of scissors
- 1 plastic cup

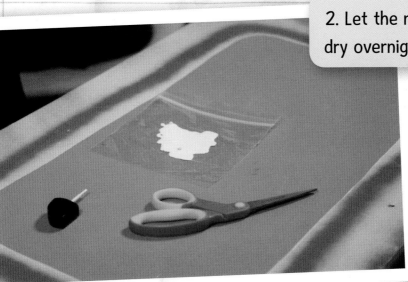

1. Pour out some white nail polish on the surface of the plastic bag in the shape of a spill.

2. Let the nail polish dry overnight.

3. Once it's dry, carefully cut the spill out.

4. Now place the fake spill and position the tipped-over cup on your friend's tablet when she's not looking. Wait for the magic to happen.

AMAZING! AND THE TABLET IS PERFECTLY FINE.

IN FACT, THE ONLY THING THAT WILL GET HURT IS YOUR FRIEND'S SIDES FROM LAUGHING SO MUCH!

BIG OL' LUMP O' COAL

Here's a sweet treat, even for someone really naughty.

YOU'LL NEED:

- 1 package sugar cookie dough
- 1 mixing bowl
- black food coloring
- 1 large spoon
- 1 baking sheet
- 1 black marker
- 1 Mason jar
- label paper
- 1 pair of scissors

HERE'S WHAT TO DO:

1. Put the cookie dough into the mixing bowl and add a few drops of black food coloring.

2. Stir until you have a nice coal color.

3. Now shape the dough into lumps and place them on the cookie sheet. (Space them a little bit apart so they don't melt together while they're baking.)

4. Have an adult place the cookies in the oven and bake them according to the package directions.

5. Trace the Mason jar lid onto the label paper.

6. Next, write LUMPS OF COAL on the label.

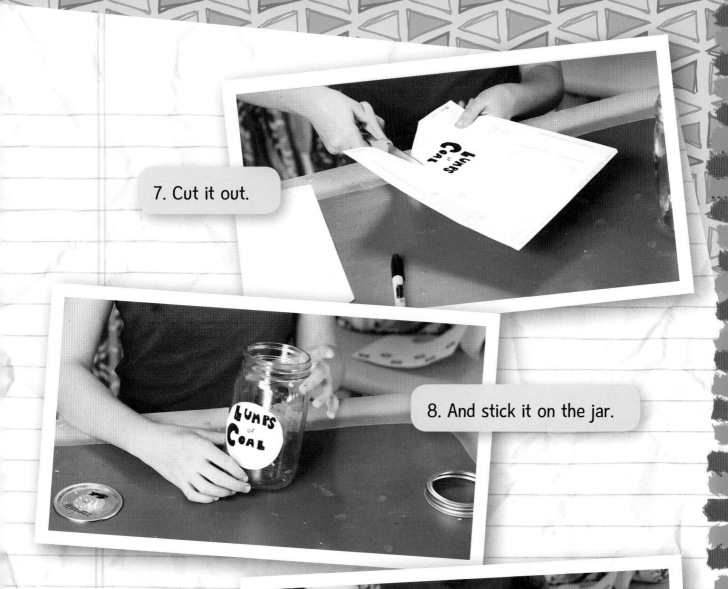

7. Cut it out.

8. And stick it on the jar.

9. After the cookies are baked and cooled, place them in the jar.

BEING NAUGHTY NEVER TASTED SO GOOD!

INVISI-PAINT

Shhh! I'm doing secret spy work. If you can keep a secret, I'll show you how to hack my Invisi-Paint.

YOU'LL NEED:

- ½ cup baking soda
- ½ cup water
- 1 small bowl
- 1 spoon
- 1 sheet of paper
- 1 paintbrush
- some grape juice

1. Place the baking soda and the water into a small bowl.

2. Mix them together. This will be your invisible paint.

195

3. On your paper, draw whatever super-secret design or message you'd like with your invisi-paint and the paintbrush. Then let it dry.

4. To reveal your secret design, brush grape juice over the painting.

TIP

Swipe off the grape juice when you begin to see the message!

SHHH!

LIVE FROM *LIFE HACKS* FOR KIDS—IT'S SUNNY!

Q: You have an amazing sense of humor on the show—is it easy for you to be funny?

A: Since I was seven years old, I've been taking improvisation classes at Studio LOL with an amazing couple named Katy and Ryan Chase. They really helped me gain confidence. I don't get nervous anymore.

I also love talking to people. I try to fit in a joke anytime I can. Even if it's not funny—I still do it!

Sometimes, it's hard to come up with stuff. Sometimes, it's stupid humor that's funny. I use a lot of puns—a *lot* of them.

HA HA HA!

Q: It sounds as though you laugh a lot with your family and friends. Is that true?

A: Yes, definitely!

Q: When you're taping the show, do you ever laugh?

A: Yes! A lot! That's why it takes so long sometimes to tape a show. We always come up with funny, embarrassing characters for me to do. So I do them, and it can be really hysterical and even obnoxious. Sometimes, we have to stop filming because one of the directors laughs out loud.

Once, while we were taping an episode, we couldn't get anything right. Gidget was on this episode with me. We did the takes over and over again. And the last time we tried it, the table we were standing behind fell over and hit the camera. No one on the set could believe it. None of us could stop laughing! It was the worst luck possible!

Q: So things can and do go wrong, but the show goes on, right?

A: Absolutely!

CONCLUSION

Life Hacks for Kids celebrated its one hundredth episode on September 10, 2016. We had a big party with cake to mark the occasion. One hundred episodes is a pretty big deal. But we are not done yet! We are continuing to work on more episodes of Life Hacks for Kids to share with you.

What's next for me? I'm still working hard in school. I love filmmaking, acting, and being a musician. I hope to continue with the arts—composing music for films, becoming a writer or an actress—or maybe all of the above! I recently started learning about special effects makeup. I just made a zombie movie and did the makeup for everyone in it. If a subject isn't taught at my school, I reach out to people in the field to guide me.

And of course I'll keep on hacking!

I hope you enjoyed creating the hacks in this book and learning more about me—it's been a blast!

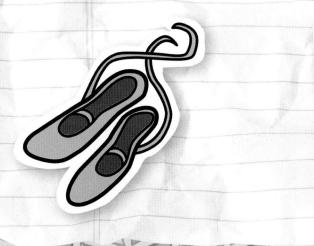

INDEX

Photos on pages 33, 34 (top), 35 (bottom), 60, 107, 108, 128 (right), 129, 130, 131, 155, 176, 177, 198, 199, and 200 courtesy of Sunny Keller.

All other photos © Dreamworks Animation Publishing LLC.

Photographer: Anthony Nex.

Written with help from Gina Shaw.

Activities based on scripts provided by DreamworksTV.